RE$PECTING ₵HANGE

Victoria McKenna-Karaniuk

Respecting Change
Copyright © 2022 Victoria McKenna-Karaniuk

Produced and printed by Stillwater River Publications.
All rights reserved. Written and produced in the
United States of America. This book may not be reproduced
or sold in any form without the expressed, written
permission of the author and publisher.

Visit our website at
www.StillwaterPress.com
for more information.

First Stillwater River Publications Edition

ISBN: 978-1-958217-90-0

1 2 3 4 5 6 7 8 9 10
Written by Victoria McKenna-Karaniuk.
Cover & interior book design by Matthew St. Jean.
Published by Stillwater River Publications,
Pawtucket, RI, USA.

*The views and opinions expressed in this book are solely
those of the author and do not necessarily reflect the views
and opinions of the publisher.*

I'd like to shout out my family, my close friends, and really everyone who's contributed to making me who I am today.

A special thank you to Christine and Brendan McKenna, my grandparents who have always supported me in my darkest times.

I'm also extremely grateful for my mother, Kara McKenna, who has always tried her hardest to keep me on a good path.

Running, stepping so quick
but my mind was moving faster.
I was on my ten toes
all the way to my car.
I remember this feeling deep within me
that something was wrong.
In my head I was all alone,
but in reality, there was someone
watching in the distance.
God was with me
but death was praying on me.
I felt like I was playing cat and mouse.
Unfortunately, I was the mouse.
I was shaking so much
I could barely hold the wheel straight.
As I stepped on the gas
I felt like it may be my last time driving so fast.

No matter the circumstance
I was still curious of the cause.
I try to follow the laws
but there's plenty who don't.
Just tell 'em they can't
and they'll be like, "ha ha I won't?"
In this life it's a game
and none feel ashamed
when it comes to their life.
A lot of the time
they don't care what the crime
as long as they're eating.
The more hungry
the more ruthless.
They'll smoke you like some crack,
hit you in the dome:
make you toothless.

Only competing with who I was yesterday.
As long as I'm alive I'll be learning.
I've seen things so sick
make your stomach start turning.
Thanks to our government
every cent I earned got me fed.
I ain't no saint.
I been misled too
but to find yourself is like dodging missiles.
When you're quick enough
feels like an angel just kissed you.
Anybody who doesn't know
gets categorized as clueless.
Can't lie
it's me in the shoes
of the one seeking to be aware.
Wholehearted and I care
to stand up for the weak it's only fair.
Nothing in this life that can scare me,
after you look death in the eyes
you realize
real lies only fool yourself.
I don't judge people by the cover,
I read vibes like a book off the shelf.

You're probably wondering
what happened to me that day.
That day I was driving too fast,
that day I thought it was my last.
I have to tell you though
I only learned lessons.
To be my own enemy
was the only reason for me stressing.
This day I learned
how important my medication is
just as valuable as my meditation is.
To get my mind right,
relax,
and tune in.

The key to life is in our hands,
these doors are ours to open.
Just depends on perception,
did what you go through strengthen you
or make you lessen?
No, that's not a trick question.
Just a genuine response would be expected.
In this land of the free
you can be whatever you want to be,
as long as you believe.
Just don't deceive
yourself by choosing less than what's best
and remember you're not alone.
There's so many with a story
just like you.
Wear the shoes you walk in proudly,
lace them up loudly.
Let anyone watching be inspired,
life's like a movie
and I'd rather be like Kevin with the heart
than cold like Michael with the myers.
I conspire to do good
now, I may be from the hood
but I'm mentally rich.
I've got a million-dollar mindset
and it's one anyone can have.
Something nobody can take away from you.
A gift so blessed
feels like God himself
breathed it into you.

The paths we're given to walk in this life aren't easy,
I remember being nine years old
being told
that my father took his own life
by a knife.
At ten
I also remember when
my uncle discussed
the type of tuff card in life
I had been dealt.
He spoke of the circumstance
but the pain I had wasn't felt.
I used to be ashamed
but the wiser I got
the more I realized that
although my dad died in vain
I'm not supposed to follow in his footsteps.
I've got my own life to live
and my own knowledge to give.

I'm still learning
I don't know it all.
I had to fight my demons
and in the end I had to fall.
To get back up wasn't easy
sometimes you have to crawl.
Just cause we take life for granted sometimes
doesn't mean we can't wake up
and thank God for it all.

At 11
I remember being so appalled.
Asking why my dad took his life
and left without a call.
It was so unexpected.
I never suspected
I would go through his pain.
The older I got the more I reflected.
This whole situation
shattered not only my heart
but my perception.
As a little girl
I didn't understand
the demons or their objectives.
I didn't understand
why it took my dad's death
for him to be accepted.
Life is short and a blessing.
It can be horrific but we have to see the light
regardless of our constant stressing.

Even when the sun doesn't shine
we know it's in the distance.
Just have to pray for better days
and genuinely want better.
Don't only use your letters to deceive.
The English language is a dialogue
we use to express what we believe.
I don't judge people for what their born into
I see who they deceive.
I've been in the wrong too
no need to pretend to be perfect.
In my book
honesty gets respect
and that's always worth it.
There's definitely more depth to these words
than just the surface.
Emotion in every word written
straight from the heart
this is my script
there's nothing in it that's bitten.

Are you living or are you racing?
I ask myself lately what is it that I'm pacing?
The pursuit of happiness isn't just a saying...
it's a constant struggle that's why I'm steady praying.
When I flashback
and start replaying that day
I get lost in reality.
Until I remember
how beautiful clarity is.
Just as much as a gift
as genuine sincerity is.
When you really only want to better yourself
and not interrupt what is:
it's a step in the right direction.
Once you realize how strong your voice is
you realize how
you can distribute the whole world affection.

The nation's oppressions
aren't something we have to entertain.
Just have to sit down with yourself and God..
let him do some tweaking in your brain.
Do we choose to
be born?
None of us have but we all have a mission to survive.

Traditions kept alive are so beautiful.
Absolutely love different cultures.
Amazing how were all unique
yet so alike.
We all share one Earth.
I mean
for what it's worth
I really care
about future generations.
Future creations
and the nearly extinct.

When I think it's deeper than the moment.
I feel my love for writing is potent.
It's a little bizarre
and a bit different
but I swear my intention
is to amuse
and get you thinking.
Enjoy a little language,
maybe use it for a hobby.
I know it's a little hoppy
but if you stick along
maybe you'll get to learn something new.
Not just about me
but maybe about you.

It's not a shame
to be proud of who you are
but to judge someone
by what their color is
or who they are
creates a lot of scars.

Separation stems
from judgment and diversity
the second is a beautiful thing
and it's time we portray
that in every university.

I know I've had moments
of being delirious
But I've realized racism and poverty
seem to be a sour subject
Like let's get serious
it's one that's real
Karma too
but people ponder
why they're so full of anger
but can't even feel.

Real depth in life
comes from being open minded.
I know
I have no idea
what this life is.
I do know wrong
from right is.
That is a gift from above
and it holds the key of life.
To really not only want the best for yourself
but for others too
is so beautiful.
Of course
do what's best for you
but be honest about greed.
People wasting so much time and money
when there's people we could feed.
I'm here to do more
than just make money and freelance.

Remember
you can't judge a book by the cover.
What you look like
doesn't define you
neither do your lovers.
I know there's so much more to us
than just trying to marry.
So many who carry this weight with them.
Yearning for a person
to call their gem.
There's infinite possibilities to our future.
I have to remember
this is my life
and it's not a movie
but I'm the producer.
We really do create our own realities.
Perception wise
we can rise
to new heights
and end casualty.

Are you honest
about the pain you deal with?
Do you throw fire to the flame
or try to find people you can heal with?
I'm not trying to come off as a saint
these are just some questions
my mind seems to paint.
I've been a fighter and a lover
can't say I'm easy to deal with but I would like to acquaint.
I'm not perfect
and it's not a myth that we evolve
I just sit back
and think about the flaws I need to solve.
Although our past doesn't define us
it surely contributes to what we see is unresolved.
To look inside is
how I began to evolve.
I stare back at my own soul.
In the mirror I see a woman
growing older but especially wiser.
I know I can be a good advisor
to those who can listen.
I sit with God
and he grants me higher intuition.
When I sit in his holy presence
everything is fluent.
I lose myself
but when I find my way back
I see how everything truly is congruent.
That is to God's plan.

We may try to withstand the prophecy
but it's coming true.
I even withdrew
from the depth of God's love
but he flew in to save me.
He knew how to call me back
no matter who tried to call me crazy.
I get scared when I think of the past me but
it's true that the Lord's forgiveness is everlasting.
I can better conduct myself.
I've been dragged to three psych units
and thought I couldn't reconstruct my health.
Even pulled on a show at twelve
to give Dr. Phil some wealth.
I made a bad decision.
I let someone get hurt
and recorded it which was so twisted.
Not everyone understood
I was a sheep.
I thank God for
changing my mentality for the better.
It took me a while to reconsider what I reap.
However, I learned young
that talk is cheap.
Had to boss up my mentality
and keep on trying to peep
what a real woman should be.
Still not quite sure exactly who I'll be in this world.
Diagnosed schizophrenic at nineteen
and that's when things began to swirl.

I'm so far from perfect.
Have to be realistic
about our characteristics.
I know I don't know it all.
Matter of fact the day I thought I did
was the day I felt the fall.
The fall into depression.
That dark mentally teaches lessons.
I have to be realistic
we're our own teacher and coach.
I'm not perfect
and I wanna change my approach.
I can be tough on myself and others.
I've smothered people and lovers
with unnecessary demands.
That's when I question my mentality.
I shouldn't expect anything but peace
and I create that in this reality.
Although I've practiced immorality
I genuinely thank Jesus for his capacity
to love.
He gives us all the seeds
we need to rise above.

People think I'm crazy
cause I feel things so strongly
and don't hide it.
It's dope to be able to feel again.
Sometimes it feels harder
when it comes time to heal again
but don't feel different,
you're no alien.
It's only human
for people to evolve.
Just depends on your situation
are there things you're tryna solve?
Sometimes we learn things
not once but twice.
Sometimes life keeps showing us
until we get it right.
Never thought it was in style
to have no emotion.
I was raised in church
and taught to have a heart.
Doesn't mean life's always perfect
I still find myself in the dark.
There's been times I've been so stressed
I didn't see hope in cleaning up my own mess.
Until I started confessing
what's really messing
with me.

My own mentality
bad habits I'm trying to repeat.
The old me is an enemy
I'm trying to defeat.
I can control my destiny
just have to believe I'm better than who I was yesterday.
It's an everyday battle
but that one is always worth the fight.
Only competing with who I've been before.
The best gift in life
is peace and that's my kind of galore.
I believe karma is real.
I've felt my fair share.
Whether good or bad
we all put it in the air.
Trying to avoid despair
and repair
the old me.
The child who still wants her dad.
It's sad to lose a parent so young.
For so many years I bit my tongue.

I still wish
I could talk to my father.
As his daughter
I grew up and was diagnosed
schizophrenic too.
Never imagined
I would go through
what he had to endure.
He was so pure to me.
Never saw an episode from him,
just love.
Truly feel like he was sent from above.
He taught me many lessons.
We'd be at the table
and he'd be pressing me.
Telling me to finish all my food.
He'd tell me how
there's many who are starving.
I think that's why
I find it so alarming.

Do you care
about what you drive
or what drives you?
I'm not asking the same question twice
try to differentiate between the two.
Life's more than the exterior or the surface.
I wake up everyday
and feel called to find a higher purpose.
I'm sick of thinking
money and escaping reality
is the only form of joy.
After years of making wrong decisions
I realized I wrongly filled a void.
I'm still not done escaping it.
I mean
I don't fill the void the same
but I'm still trying hard
to avoid the pit.
The pit of despair.

When people work their whole lives away
to see they only cared about what they wear.
When everything is gone
what are we left with?

Our souls are behind the surface.
All this designer and loud music
makes it hard to find our purpose.
I feel the lord works through me.
I'm a fellow sinner
and we can make the best army for him.
The lord is my witness
and I owe it all to him.
We're all capable of feeling his light.
Even the worst of days
can be ended
with the best insight.
Ever since I took Gods hands
I can't stop flight.

That is to a higher mental latitude.
I need to practice with more gratitude
and prayer.
The most scary times in my life
were when I focused on the darkness.
Although it's all around us,
within we hold a fountain of light.
That's how I made it through
the fight for my life.
So happy I realized
I didn't need a brand-new car
to be happy.
My outlook on life
was really crappy
but I'm so happy
that's the past me.
I still have hard days
and shed tears.
But I'm so happy
that the years are always changing
for the better.
Even when the weather is foggy
I know brighter days do exist.
As I persist
I should get the gist
of how to maintain peace.
At least I pray I can.
Not sure if I can withstand
another episode.

Scary to lose your own mind.
It took some time
to find myself again.
I still feel lost.
the sauce is thick.
I mean the environment we live in
gets hectic.

I beg God to please keep me on the right path.
I've felt the devil's wrath
but it's not something I can let just pull me in.
It's a daily task trying not to sin.
Listening to the good voice within
I realize I always have more reflecting to begin.
I know I need more peace.
I need more love.
I need more of God in my life.
I've been in strife
on many occasions.
Maybe it's my location:
maybe it's me.
I don't know,
sometimes I feel blind I can't see.
That is back to reality.
Months spent in a fog.
After that day in the car
I didn't know if I could even jog.
That dark mentality caused depression.
Crazy to think how much we'd relate,
tears stream down my face.
Thinking of what we could have discussed.
How tough this life is.
We could've got through it together.
We could've stormed through the weather.

I appreciate everyone
that's been there for me,
even those who've tried
to put fear in me.
It participated in helping me
see the reality in my mentality.
Every circumstance and hardship
I appreciate because of how much
it contributed to my progression.
No matter what people say about me
I won't let it make me lessen.
I learned young that's a fools way to be
less than what's best for some revenge.
That's a waste of time and
back and forth violence
usually will never end.
Til one steps up and
decides to really be
the bigger person.
I'm not who I was
a couple years ago
and I thank God
for not letting me worsen.
I may have back tracked before
and it's okay when that happens.
Life always guides me back to you
when I call that's real compassion.
Constantly asking God
for his presence, peace, and patience.

Without these I realize
I'm uncontrollably complacent.
Daily pacing even in my head.
I dread the mentality
of not making my dreams reality.
I see it all the time.
I know there's meaning in every life
and we have a voice for a reason.

So thankful for the bees and the birds.
even the lemons & the curds.
I've had real sour days,
even some wicked ways
but I still stay
trying to pursue a better way.
It's not a joke to be a good person..
I don't know why I ever let the world lessen me.
I had to step up to myself
and realize I was my own enemy.
Not once, not twice,
but multiple occasions.
So many nights I was gazing at the stars
asking why they're so amazing.

I know we have a higher purpose.
The fate of our future
doesn't have to rely on old ties with our past.
Every day is not just a gift
but it could be our last.
Really not a joke
how precious life is.
I don't know what heightens some egos
to believe they're above another person.
We have more in common
than a lot realize
and it's actually concerning.
Not the fact we're all alike
but the fact people would rather create division.
Communication is a given provision.
When we listen,
not just to reply,
that's how we understand
how to live in another man's shoes.

I can't get over the fact
that we don't choose to be born.
Don't get me wrong,
I really believe that life is a gift.
I just think that some people
need to shift their view
from thinking so wickedly.
We have tools we can use
to create peace within
and I swear I never want to take them for granted again.
Meditation and prayer
was so rare in my life
so many scars
my heart has been torn with a knife.

Through solitude and gratitude
I reached my mental destination.
Now I know the way through my mind.
The old place where I used to be confined
is no longer where I want my presence.
I've been trying to learn
to be a better person since my adolescence.
Courage comes from change
and because of that I'm so happy
for everything in my past.
If it wasn't for the last thing I did
I wouldn't be thinking like this.
Any step in the right direction
even if it's through the mud.

Words aren't just to be used
to create an illusion and to deceive.
Manipulation is so cruel
and it's a sabotage no one should receive.

The more I self-evaluate
the more I see how we're equal.
Life is a neverending prequel
and I wanna be everything I desire.
The old me wanted expensive things
but now I wanna help people grow higher.
I definitely believe words
can change someone's life.
Like when I heard a knife
supposedly took my dad's life.
They've changed mine since a child.
I know it's been a while
since I was so little
but I could never forget.
I miss when I believed
all adults cared if a child were upset.
Now that I've grown up
I see people aging out of sympathy.
That never made sense to me.
Is empathy based off age?
Or should I flip the page?

Seems like it's something nobody wants to talk about
but it's really happening.
I care enough to stand up
for what I see is saddening.
I know what it's like to feel all alone.
It's not a good place to be.
I ran into the arms of people
who didn't deserve me.
All along I was searching to fill a void.
That was a truth I'd avoid
but I self-analyze at the end of every day.
I may not be perfect
but I truly confess my wrongs anyway.
That's what makes me strong.
Realizing my weaknesses
keeps me self-aware.
I swear
I never felt peace
until I asked God to repair me.
That's when I was able to care enough
about my weary heart.
Ever since the start
it hadn't been easy.
I mean this life can get greasy.
You know it gets messy and stressed
situations be constantly addressed.

So blessed
but still get lost sometimes.
I know I got some rhymes
and this flow soothes my soul.
Maybe it could play a role
in doing the same for another human.
I'm assuming I can't be the only one.
Do you and your friends
believe in your ability to evolve?
Teamwork really can make the dream work
and there's problems we can solve.

To create the life I deserve
was once a joke to me.
Until I asked God to tap in.
I had days I didn't think it was possible.
but just like Kim Possible
I had to make it happen.
"With God anything is possible"
Is one of my favorite quotes.
I swear when we're sick
he holds the true antidotes.
Like I said
I was diagnosed schizophrenic at nineteen.
I thought I'd be another statistic
but I fought through the scenes.
Life kept throwing me thriller and horror
but I needed peace.
I used to crave escape
but now I try to increase my knowledge of the streets.
Mental stamina is what makes a fighter have a heart.
I've waisted tears and many years
fighting out the dark.
Until I realized it doesn't end here
unless we put the car in park.

I've always wanted to go fast
but I'm learning to stay within the limit.
Casually drifting past the pivot.
It's a different time we're living in.
Young soul with an old heart.
Or a young heart with an old soul
shouldn't we recognize who's really in control?

I know there's a higher power.
I used to be scared to talk about
God but now I see the hour.
"Ask and you shall receive"
I wanna talk about this one
because it makes me think how we deceive.
I mean I've deceived myself.
I put my trust on the shelf
and even thought it was right.
Until I went into nature
and asked God to show me
how to see like a kite.
His view is above all.
He taught me how to stand tall
even as a sinner.
I may be young but I'm no beginner
in life.
I give it all to my father
because he was sacrificed by a knife.
I was poked at too.
My heart torn
and my blood would boil like a hot stew.
Young and full of confusion
until I ran into the light.
I realized I needed to be there.
I loved it until I ran into spite.
I was scared.
Petrified to live in righteousness.
I cowered from expressing the word

and hid in the dark.
Until I felt the spark
in me come back.
I knew I didn't lack what I needed.
The seed you planted was heated.
It was ready to grow.
I didn't understand the darkness
until my fingers touched the holy warm glow.
I know I'm not a super human.
It's actually amusing
people accusing me of being off drugs.
Just because I have special abilities
doesn't mean you don't have the same type of proximities.
I keep on trying to escape the susceptibility
of my disability.
swear it's a disease.
That's why I love God so much
He sets my mind at ease.
When I drift away from him
that's when my heart starts to freeze.

Growing up in New England
I didn't always understand the seasons.
But as I got older
I realized how nature has its reasons.
I'm talking about respecting change.
animals and plants rearranged
themselves for millions of years.
They don't kill or shed tears on purpose.
But we all know what's done to them at the circus.
As humans we have the ability
to solve and evolve
just as animals do.
I feel we should do it better
but there's still innocent lives being abused.
I don't mind sitting around a table
and talking about what isn't easy.
It's when people can't be realistic
that doesn't please me.
I've been trying to divert from a false reality.
I need my perception to be only full of clarity.

I always lived by the expression
follow your heart.
Until I got myself
nailed to a circumstance
just like a dart.
I thought I'd be tied to the past
but a part of me said no
that's not what it has to be.
Even through the darkness
we can come out and find prosperity.
Just gotta check my speed and direction.

My destination depends on the correlation of my thoughts.
That's a tricky process and it takes a lot of watts.
It's always good to have a plot
but what's the moral of the story?
Mine is as deep as everlasting life
and I wanna spread the glory.
I just feel my experiences taught me a lot.
I don't know it all but I thought I'd tell y'all.

I'm not perfect
but I knew I was worthy of God's love.
I know
because I cried to him alone
and he heard me from above.
Everything beautiful in me
comes from him.
Grateful to see the sunlight
even when the sky is grim.
I didn't always feel like that
and sometimes I withdrew.
I backed away from my faith
and that was a mistake
I wish I never knew.
I mean
I'm so grateful I realized
but it's a shame it had to happen.
I'll still take the good from it
and see if I can avoid my own madness.

I agree to make myself a better future.
I know I can tutor myself to be the best person.
There's so many people
who came from darkness and made art.
That's a part of me I need to express.
I felt like I couldn't move sometimes
and that's how I knew I was depressed.
I always loved to dance.
I always had big dreams
but I can't say the same about my self-esteem.
I didn't know if I could make things happen.
Until my passion met my drive
and I became alive.
I felt God show me his way.
I felt like a stray cat
looking for love
until our Heavenly Father heard from above.
When push comes to shove
I wanna be full of love.

I had to be more aware of what I was reaping.
The truth was seeping
with regret.
I know I tend to forget
what I've done wrong
but there's a song
in me that wants me
to be free.
It's from God
and he calls out for you and me.
He wants us to understand that any sin
can be forgiven by him.
We just have to swear to live by the word.
I mean it's not unheard
of that people feel the light
and it changes their lives.

My mind constantly flashes back to the past.
I'm not a fan of it.
I even ran from it.
I mean not necessarily from circumstances
but from thoughts.
I sit back and wonder
what it really costs to be a boss.
I know I've made plenty of wrong decisions
but they don't define me.
I actually still have a lot to leave behind me.
I just have to ask God to remind me.
I know he's answered questions
but now it's time to find me.
When I say that I mean my purpose,
please don't be confused by the rhyming.
I just like to talk in a way that heals my mind.

I'm not perfect yet
but I'm gonna stay on the grind.
Money is a necessity
but peace of mind is what's worth the real chase.
Remember it's never a waste
to sit down and express how you feel.
maybe run a mile
or take the time to kneel.
Prayer does a lot for me
and I tend to forget.
I wonder what I should do next
and even feel regret.
That's not a good feeling someone should sit in forever.
When I level out my thoughts
I remember the weather always changes.
Gotta remember there's more than just exchanges.
More than just money to chase.
I want to touch hearts and be the face
that helps the entire race
come together.
I mean even a feather
or a butterfly
can change the world right?
Why not take flight?
I'm not quite sure
what makes each individual happy
but I'll dare to share
what has helped me.

Even if it's not my taste
I'll still try to digest it.
Sometimes my ego
gets the best of my senses
but I'll still try to relinquish
the English that doesn't subside
with my dream future.
I'll extinguish all the bridges I burned.
I've heard the expression
to turn the other cheek.
wow this one really turned.
I'm proud of who I've become.
Proud to know
it's not about where you're from.
That doesn't define anyone.
Where you wanna go in life says it all.

Lived in subsidized housing
but that doesn't make anyone a loser.
They say beggars can't be choosers
but not everyone got the body to work at hooters.
Some disabled and I mean even mentally.
I know what's it's like to be out of work.
I know what it's like to rely on the government,
I know what it's like to twerk.
Everyone is built differently
and in the land of the free
we should help one another make survival work.
I'm trying to focus on the future.
I like to talk.
I think I could be a tutor.
Not at stuff like math
but maybe with life.
I want to show people
God can chisel at a heart of ice.
Don't concise with your past
and let your last
sin keep you on a leash.
Just ask God
in Jesus' name
and capeesh,
it's done.
Maybe not right away
but through God's son,
we ask and we receive.
This isn't just some words,

this is a message sent for us to believe.
I've felt the power of the Holy Spirit, have you?
Even if you haven't yet
just ask and he'll come unto you.

Ever since a youngin'
ever since a jit,
I was taught to break bread
that's just how we split.
I love to learn;
I love to grow.
Since a youngin',
since a pho
I've been trying
to get more than dough.
I want true peace.
Yes, stability But
that happiness that can't be bought.
I fought for my respect
and I neglected to love myself.
I used to work like a dog
and realized it's not always good
to shove oneself.
I mean not so hard
to the point you feel scarred.
I want to learn many life lessons.
I don't know it all
like I said I still be stressing.
I know it feels good
to share knowledge and wealth.
When I speak I speak for myself.

At 20 I was Re-diagnosed.
Could toast to the fact
I don't have hallucinations.
Scary to lose your mind
and have that kind of imagination.
They said I was manic bipolar.
The older I
get the more I felt my heart getting pulled out like a molar.
The doctor said she's proud of me
and that is when I told her I can't lie.
So many issues.
Plenty of tears cried,
plenty of tissues
and this news was still new to me.
I mean I'm only 22.
Right now life's teaching me
how to be alone.
I know how to love
but there's so many people made of stone.
I feel like I've condoned abuse for too many years.
I've cried too many tears
caused by people who supposedly loved me.
I just keep on striving
to find a better purpose.
I know I'm not worthless.

Life is not easy
and I've had the shit end of the stick.
I like to keep the fire in me burning
and this is the type of stuff that'll make a flick.

CPSIA information can be obtained
at www.ICGtesting.com
Printed in the USA
LVHW040058230323
742312LV00002B/19

9 781958 217900